The *The* **EARTH** *and* **SPACE**

MAKING SENSE *of* SCIENCE

Peter Riley

A⁺
Smart Apple Media

First published in 2004 by Franklin Watts
96 Leonard Street, London EC2A 4XD

Franklin Watts Australia
45–51 Huntley Street, Alexandria NSW 2015

Series editor: Rachel Cooke, Editor: Kate Newport,
Art director: Jonathan Hair, Designer: Mo Choy

Picture credits:
Mark Antman/Image Works/Topham: 4t.
Bettmann/Corbis: 7c.
British Museum, London/Topham: 17b.
Dennis de Cicco/Still Pictures: 24.
Myron J. Dorf/Corbis: 26t.
ESA/PLI/Corbis: front cover main image.
Mary Evans Picture Library: 23b.
Frozen Images/Image Works/Topham: 5bl.
Aaron Horowitz/Corbis: 20.
NASA: front cover inset l & r, 6t, 22, 26b, 27b, 29c.
NASA/Corbis: 21b.
Douglas Peebles/Corbis: 6b.
Picturepoint/Topham: 5tr, 9t, 9c, 18, 19br.
John Sandford/SPL: 15bl, 16t.
Science Museum, London/HIPS/Topham: 11c.
Charles Walker/Topham: 8bl, 12b, 13c.

All other photography by Ray Moller.

Published in the United States by Smart Apple Media
2140 Howard Drive West, North Mankato, Minnesota 56003

Library of Congress Cataloging-in-Publication Data

Riley, Peter D.
The Earth and space / by Peter Riley.
p. cm. — (Making sense of science)
Includes index.
ISBN 1-58340-713-8
1. Astronomy—Juvenile literature. 2. Solar system—Juvenile literature. I. Title.

QB46.R57 2005
520—dc22   2004056550

2 4 6 8 9 7 5 3 1

CONTENTS

THE TURNING EARTH

We are standing on a huge, rocky ball called Earth. We can't feel it, but it is continually turning in space. As it turns, one side of it faces toward the sun, and the other side faces away. When the part that we are living on is facing the sun, we call it day, and when we are facing away, it is night.

The sun appears to rise and set, but these movements are due to the way Earth turns.

As our part of the Earth turns toward the sun, we see the sky change from black to blue. Also during the day, as the Earth continues to turn, the sun appears to move across the sky in a curved path.

MAKE A MODEL SKY

Making models helps us understand how scientists use experiments to formulate and test their ideas. We can make a model of the sky by taking a bowl of water and putting a drop of milk in it. Droplets of milk spread out in the water like dust in the air. If you shine a flashlight into your model sky, you should see it turn slightly blue due to the way the droplets scatter the light. This shows us why the sky looks blue.

WHY THE SKY IS BLUE

John Tyndall (1820–1893) was an Irish scientist who investigated why the sky was blue. He studied how light beams passed through the air and how they were affected by particles of dust that were present. He knew that sunlight was made from all the colors we see in the rainbow. He believed that the daytime sky was blue because dust particles in the air scattered the blue color in the light from the sun.

THE NIGHT SKY

At night, when our part of the Earth is turned away from the sun, we can see dimmer objects that are hidden by the sun's glare during the day.

These objects are various planets of the solar system and stars in the rest of the universe. At different times of the year, we can see different stars and planets as our position around the sun changes.

Stars look like small points of twinkling light, while planets appear larger and shine steadily.

Living things adapt to changes in the seasons. This tree loses its leaves in the fall and winter and grows new ones in the spring. This helps it survive the cold winter.

THE FOUR SEASONS

The turning Earth is also moving in another way; it is moving around the sun. As it makes its journey, different parts of the Earth receive different amounts of sunlight, causing what we call the seasons.

MAKING SENSE

We can see the sun, the stars, and the planets in the sky, and we can explain them because of what we have been told. In the past, people explained things differently. Some ancient people thought the night sky was a dark, overturned bowl with holes in it. The light that shone through it was believed to come from heaven. Many people saw pictures in the sky and grouped the stars to make objects, animals, or people. Seasons were explained through actions of the gods—not the movement of the Earth. However, since ancient times, scientists called astronomers have studied the night sky and made calculations and predictions. Slowly, they established the knowledge we have today of the Earth and space.

SPHERES IN SPACE

Today, we know that Earth is a sphere in space, but no one was really sure of this until the middle of the 20th century. It was then that rockets carrying cameras were launched into space and it became possible to take pictures from beyond Earth's atmosphere.

A view of Earth taken from a ▮ spacecraft on its way to the moon.

THE SURFACE OF THE EARTH

In early times, many people believed that Earth was flat. However, if this were true, a person would see the same stars in the sky wherever he traveled. The ancient Greeks noticed that as a person traveled north, new stars came into view, while more familiar stars in the south disappeared. This led them to believe that the surface of the Earth was curved in the shape of a sphere.

A second observation also helped people believe that Earth had a curved surface. When ships sail away, they get smaller, but when they reach the horizon, the lower part disappears first, and then the upper part. If the Earth was flat, they would just continue to become smaller and smaller.

DOES THE MOON CHANGE SHAPE?

We see the moon by sunlight reflected off its surface. Sometimes the moon appears to be a disk, then half a disk, and at other times a crescent. We see these different shapes because different amounts of the moon are being lit at different times. The rest of the moon is still there, but we cannot see it because it is in shadow. These different shapes of the moon are called "phases."

As these ships sail over the horizon, the last thing to be seen will be the tops of their masts.

HOW DO THEY SHINE?

Make the room dark. Hold a spherical object and a flashlight at arm's length and shine the light onto the sphere. Shine the light from different angles and look at the light areas and shaded areas. Do the same thing with a disk, a cylinder, and a cube and compare the light reflecting from their surfaces. You will see that only the sphere shows shapes like the phases of the moon.

An early illustration showing Galileo demonstrating his discoveries.

OBSERVING SPHERES

Galileo Galilei (1564–1642) was an Italian scientist who conducted many studies on forces and the night sky. He knew that the phases of the moon were due to the way the sun shone on its spherical shape. When he used a telescope to observe Venus, he found that it had phases too and concluded that it must also be spherical.

Galileo also looked at the sun with his telescope (a person should never do this) and saw that there were spots on its surface. The spots appeared to move and change shape just like spots on a ball when it is turned. From this, Galileo reasoned that the sun must be a sphere turning in space.

MODEL SUNSPOTS

Draw or stick dark oval shapes on a yellow ball or grapefruit. Hold it at arm's length and turn it slowly so that the spots move from left to right. Notice that as the spots come into sight, move across your view, and then disappear, they seem to change shape. This is what Galileo observed on the sun.

THE SUN IN THE SKY

As the Earth spins around, the sun appears to move across the sky in the following way. It rises over the eastern horizon, moves in a curved path across the sky, rises to its highest point at midday, then sinks down and eventually disappears below the western horizon.

Not only does the sun appear to move from east to west in this way, but it also follows different paths at different times of the year. In the summer, it rises high in the sky, but in the winter, it is lower. This is due to the way the Earth tilts (see page 14).

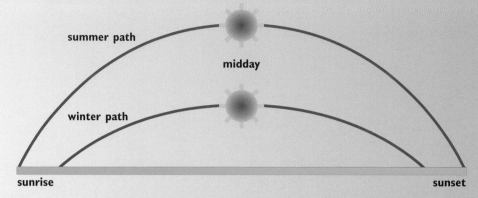

EGYPTIAN SUN GOD

The ancient Egyptians believed that the sun was a god called Ra and that he made his journey across the sky every day in a solar boat.

▮ Ra is depicted in his boat with a disk on his head in this ancient Egyptian picture.

As the sun appears to move across the sky, shadows are cast when light shines on objects on the ground. The changing length of these shadows shows how the sun travels in a curved path. In the past, before the invention of clocks, shadows were used to tell time.

◣ PLOTTING THE SUN'S PATH IN THE SKY

On a sunny morning, set up a stick in open ground. Put a stone at the top of the stick's shadow. Keep coming back to the stick every hour and putting other stones at the top of each of the shadows.

Light travels in straight lines from the sun, so the position of the shadow shows you how the position of the sun in the sky changes. At the end of the day, you should see that the stones make a curve, showing that the sun traveled in a curved path.

The observatory in Greenwich where Flamsteed measured the positions of the stars. The Meridian runs through it.

John Flamsteed (1646–1719) was an English astronomer who measured the positions of the stars at his observatory at Greenwich in London, England. In honor of his work, when maps of the world were made using vertical lines called meridians of longitude, the prime meridian of zero degrees on the map was positioned to run through Greenwich. This is now known as the Greenwich Meridian.

LOCATING YOUR POSITION

John Harrison (1693–1776), an Englishman, invented a clock that could keep time very accurately as it traveled across the sea on a ship. This allowed sailors to use Flamsteed's meridians, which indicated time differences around the world, to find their longitude.

The position of the sun could be used in the following way: the sailors noted when the sun was at its highest point in the sky. This was midday, or 12:00 noon. They then looked at the clock, which was set to the time at the Greenwich Meridian. If they noted that it was 1:00 P.M. at Greenwich, there was therefore a time difference of one hour. This meant there was a difference of 15 degrees of longitude, and they knew that they were 15 degrees longitude away from Greenwich.

Since places to the east of a point on Earth always see the sun first, the sailors knew that as it was 1:00 P.M. at Greenwich, Greenwich must be to the east of them

A portrait of John Harrison. He was a clock-maker rather than a scientist.

and they were 15 degrees west of Greenwich. If it was only 11:00 A.M. in Greenwich when the sailors recorded midday, the sailors knew that they were 15 degrees east of Greenwich.

THE SPINNING EARTH

Today, we know that Earth is spinning. One complete spin takes 24 hours, and we call this a day. For most of history, almost everyone believed that Earth did not move. There were two main reasons for this. First, we cannot feel ourselves moving. Second, the movement of the sun and stars would look the same whether the Earth was spinning or everything in the universe was spinning around the Earth.

MAKE YOUR HEAD A PLANET

Sit in a swivel chair. Close your left eye and think of your head as the planet Earth and your view with your right eye as your view of the sky. Ask a friend to hold up a yellow ball as a model sun to your left and then swivel around on your chair staring ahead. See the sun pass across your sky.

Now stay still and ask your friend to move, carrying the ball across your field of view in the same direction as it appeared to move before. Both views of your sky show a moving sun, but which method involves the biggest movement? (Note: Never look directly at the real sun. This can damage your eyes.)

SIMPLE EXPLANATIONS

William of Occam (1280–1349), an English monk, suggested that a person should always first look for a simple explanation rather than a complicated one. This idea helped scientists in the past realize that it was simpler to think of the Earth spinning around in the universe in 24 hours rather than the whole universe spinning around Earth.

WHY DON'T WE FLY OFF INTO SPACE?

One of the reasons people argued against the spinning Earth idea was because they thought that only one force could act on an object at any one time. For example, it was believed that when a cannonball was fired, it went in a straight line away from the cannon due to the force it received, and then fell straight down due to the pull of gravity.

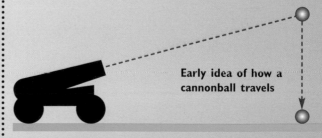

Early idea of how a cannonball travels

This meant that if Earth was spinning, its turning force would throw everything off into space, as gravity could not act to stop it.

Galileo showed that more than one force acted on the cannonball at the same time: a pushing force sent the ball off in a particular direction, but gravity was acting on it all the time as well. The effect of these two forces was to make the cannonball fall more gradually, in a curve.

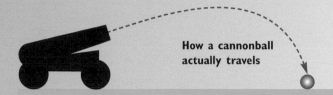

How a cannonball actually travels

The discovery that more than one force could be acting at once had huge implications. Scientists realized that everything, including the air, could move about on Earth and also be turned by the planet's spinning force without being thrown off into space.

WHICH MOVES FASTER?

Push two matchsticks into an orange—one toward the top and one on the side—and spin the orange. The top stick should spin around faster. The way places spin at different speeds on a sphere helped scientists discover that Earth actually spins.

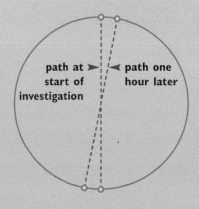

The paths taken by the swinging pendulum are shown on the floor beneath it.

path at start of investigation ► ◄ path one hour later

PROVING **ROTATION**

Jean Foucault (1819–1868), a French physicist, noticed that if a pendulum is set in motion, it will keep moving to and fro in the same direction even if its support becomes twisted around. He set up a 62-pound (28 kg) metal ball on a 200-foot (60 m) wire and made it swing in a north-south direction. The bottom of the ball had a spike that scratched a line in the sand to show the direction of swing. After an hour, the direction shown on the floor had moved clockwise by 11 degrees. When scientists thought about Earth as a spinning sphere and made calculations about it, Foucault's measurement matched their predictions exactly. The change in direction of the pendulum was exactly what should happen if Earth was spinning.

THE SOLAR SYSTEM

Earth does not just spin around on its own in space; it also moves in a path around the sun. This path is called Earth's orbit. Earth is not alone in traveling around the sun. Eight other planets have similar paths that are separated by enormous distances in space. They also move in the same direction around the sun. It has taken astronomers thousands of years to establish this knowledge.

There are other parts to the solar system as well. They are home to asteroids and comets (see page 20–21).

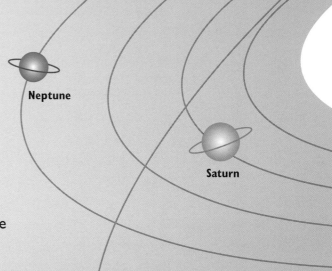

Neptune

Saturn

TRAVELING THROUGH SPACE

Earth is traveling at 6,500 miles (10,400 km) per hour around the sun. How far does it travel through space in (a) a school day of seven hours or (b) a whole day of 24 hours?

EARLY IDEAS ON THE UNIVERSE

The ancient Greeks believed that Earth was the center of the universe. The sun, moon, planets, and stars all moved around Earth. They were held in place by crystal spheres. However, some of the planets did not move steadily across the sky and sometimes appeared to move backward! A Greek astronomer named Ptolemy (A.D. 90–168) suggested that the planets move in small circles within their spheres.

The Copernican view of the universe.

Nicolaus Copernicus (1473–1543) was a Polish astronomer. He believed Ptolemy's idea was too complicated. He suggested that the sun was the center of the universe and that Earth moved in a path around the sun. Earth traveled in a circular orbit like the other planets, but everything was held in place by crystal spheres as the ancient Greeks believed.

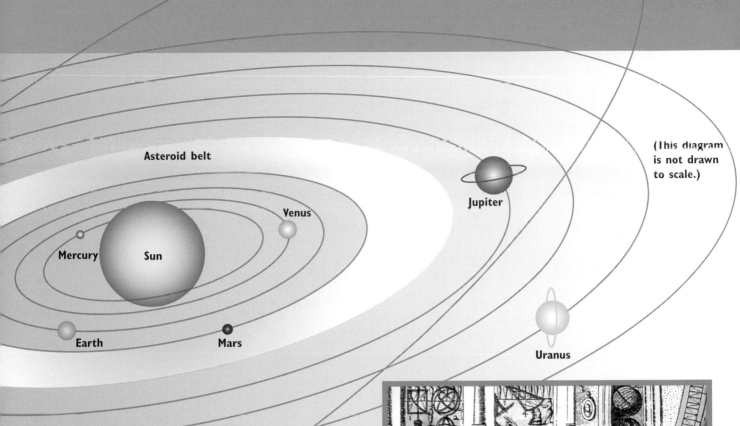

Asteroid belt

Venus

Jupiter

Mercury

Sun

Earth

Mars

Uranus

(This diagram is not drawn to scale.)

Pluto

SHATTERING **CRYSTAL SPHERES**

An artist's impression of Tycho Brahe framed by a quadrant.

Tycho Brahe (1546–1601) was a Danish astronomer. With no telescope (which had not yet been invented), he measured the angles of stars, planets, and comets above the horizon using a quadrant. Brahe used the measurements he collected to prove a comet (previously thought to be a cloud in the atmosphere) was, in fact, farther away than the moon and that its path crossed those of the planets. This meant that it could move where the crystal spheres were supposed to be. The only way to explain the path of the comet was to get rid of the crystal spheres idea.

Johannes Kepler (1571–1630) was Tycho's assistant. When Tycho died, Kepler studied the information that Tycho had collected on the orbit of Mars. He tried to plot an orbit and found that it would not fit in a circle. After testing many ideas, he found that the data showed that Mars had an elliptical orbit, not a circular one. He found that all the planets had elliptical orbits, and so the idea of movement using spheres was wrong. In the modern picture of the solar system shown above, the planets are shown moving in elliptical orbits.

MOVING AROUND THE SUN

Earth takes a year to move in its orbit around the sun. As it makes its journey, it spins once on its axis each day. The axis around which Earth spins is tilted at an angle of 23.66 degrees. The direction in which Earth tilts stays the same all the way around its orbit. This means that at a certain time of year, the Northern Hemisphere (NH) is tipped toward the sun, and the Southern Hemisphere (SH) is tipped away from it. Then, as Earth continues to move, their positions are reversed.

THE SEASONS

As Earth moves in its orbit, places have long periods of certain weather conditions. These periods are called seasons. In the tropical regions closer to the equator, there are usually two seasons: wet and dry. Farther north or south, there are four seasons: winter, spring, summer, and fall.

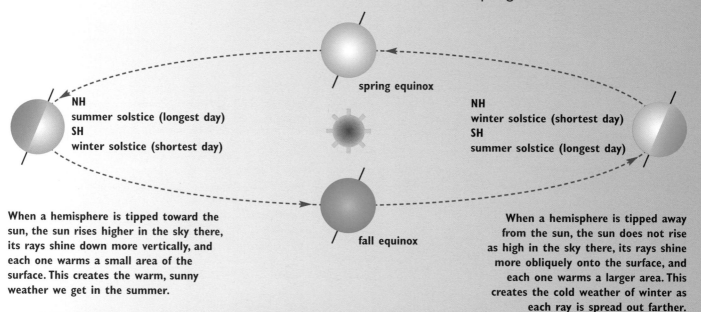

spring equinox

NH
summer solstice (longest day)
SH
winter solstice (shortest day)

NH
winter solstice (shortest day)
SH
summer solstice (longest day)

fall equinox

When a hemisphere is tipped toward the sun, the sun rises higher in the sky there, its rays shine down more vertically, and each one warms a small area of the surface. This creates the warm, sunny weather we get in the summer.

When a hemisphere is tipped away from the sun, the sun does not rise as high in the sky there, its rays shine more obliquely onto the surface, and each one warms a larger area. This creates the cold weather of winter as each ray is spread out farther.

WHY WE MOVE AROUND THE SUN

The work of Kepler and Brahe showed that Earth moved in an elliptical orbit around the sun, but it was Sir Isaac Newton (1642–1727) who first explained why this happened.

It is believed that Newton found the way to explain how gravity worked when he saw an apple fall from a tree. Newton wondered if the force that pulled on the apple also pulled on the moon and made it go around Earth. He found that he was correct. The moon was pulled around Earth by the gravitational force between Earth and the moon.

Newton also showed that each planet moved around the sun due to the gravitational force between it and the sun. He suggested this force existed throughout the universe and expressed his ideas in the Law of Universal Gravitation.

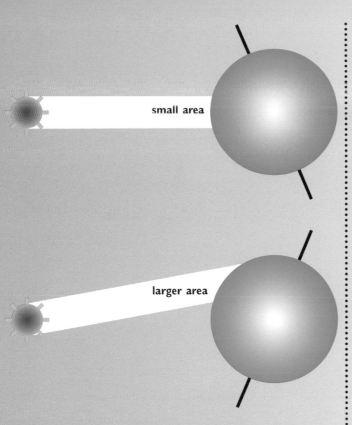

small area

larger area

COMPARING SUN RAYS

Shine a flashlight onto the surface of a ball so that the beam is almost perpendicular to the surface. Notice the size of the area that is lit up. Now shine the flashlight at an oblique angle and see how the size of the area that is lit up changes.

TRAVEL AROUND THE SUN

Hold up a ball or a lamp to make a model sun. Then have a friend hold a globe so that it tilts slightly toward the sun. Now move the globe around the sun, keeping it tilted in the same direction. Notice how each hemisphere tips toward and away from the sun as you make your journey.

USING THE **SKY** FOR **PREDICTIONS**

As Earth moves around its path, different stars appear in the night sky. Ancient peoples found that they could use the appearance of stars to predict how the conditions on Earth would change. For example, the Egyptians knew that when the star Sirius appeared in the night sky, the Nile River would flood and supply water for their crops.

Sirius is the brightest star in the sky and can be seen from most places on Earth.

THE MOON

The moon moves in an orbit around Earth. Together, Earth and the moon move around the sun. As the moon moves around Earth, the same half of it is always turned toward us. The amount of this surface that is lit by the sun changes as the moon moves in its orbit.

When the surface of the moon that faces Earth also faces the sun, we see a bright white disk—a full moon. When this surface faces away from the sun and toward the Earth, we do not see it. This is called a new moon. The new moon is more commonly, but inaccurately, used to describe the bright crescent shape in the sky that appears just after a true new moon. As the moon moves in its orbit, the area of its surface lit by the sun changes. Each area is known as a "phase" of the moon. When the phases increase in size each night, the moon is said to be waxing. When phases decrease in size each night, the moon is said to be waning.

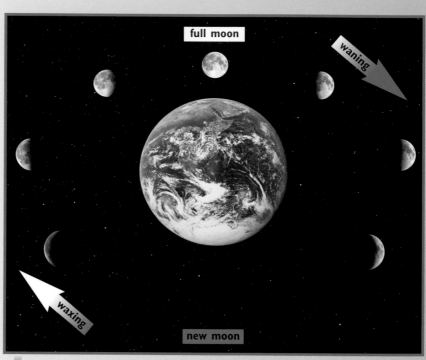

This picture shows the major phases of the moon.

MOVING IN ORBIT

Ask a friend to hold a ball in the center of the room. This represents the sun. Hold a globe so that it tilts correctly toward the sun. Ask another friend to hold a small ball (the moon) close to the model Earth. Walk slowly with the globe around the sun while your friend and the model moon move around you. Can you make a complete orbit of the sun?

WAXING OR WANING?

Look at the moon on three nights in one week. Look at the phases of the moon pictured here. Can you tell if it is waxing or waning? Check a calendar to see if you're right.

FIGURING OUT OUR YEAR

The phases tell us that the moon takes 29.5 days to go around Earth. The period of time measured by the moon in this way is called a month—from new moon to new moon.

THE CALENDAR YEAR

Unfortunately, the number of months measured by the moon does not match the time taken for Earth to travel around the sun (a year). Twelve "moonths," or lunar months, are 11 days short of a year. The Egyptians solved this problem by making each month 30 days and adding five feast days to make a 365-day year. The Romans also had to adjust their calender (see panel to the right). However, Earth actually takes 365.25 days to travel around the sun. In 1582, Pope Gregory set up a calendar in which there is an extra day every fourth year.

Augustus Caesar, the first Roman emperor. August was named after him.

The early Roman calendar had 10 months. This made a calendar of only 304 days. Since Earth takes more than 60 days longer than this to travel around the sun, the first month began 60 days earlier each year, which led to great confusion. Two more months were later added. This made a calendar of only 355 days, so Julius Caesar added an extra day to some months to make 365 days. Some of the months were named after Roman gods or rulers.

Month	Named after
Januarius	Janus, the god of gateways or beginnings and endings
Februarius	Februs, the festival of purification and cleaning
Martius	Mars, the god of war
Aprilis	Aphrilis, another name for Aphrodite, the goddess of love
Maius	Maia, the goddess of spring and growth
Junius	Juno, the goddess of wisdom and marriage
Julius	Julius Caesar, the Roman ruler
Augustus	Augustus Caesar, the nephew and successor to Julius Caesar
September	seventh month of first calendar
October	eighth month of first calendar
November	ninth month of first calendar
December	tenth month of first calendar

SOLAR AND LUNAR ECLIPSES

When most people think of an eclipse, they think of an eclipse of the sun, but there is also an eclipse of the moon. In an eclipse of the sun, the moon passes in front of the sun and stops light from reaching Earth. This happens because of an unusual coincidence. The sun is 400 times larger than the moon, but it is 400 times farther away from Earth. This means that when the moon passes in front of the sun, it completely covers it, even though it is 400 times smaller.

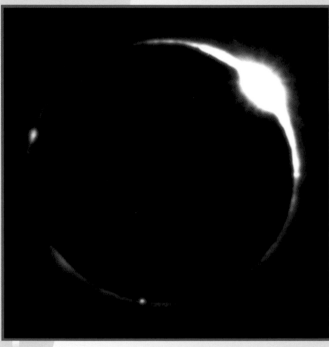

This stage of a solar eclipse is called the diamond ring effect and is caused by sunlight shining between mountains on the moon.

An eclipse of the sun occurs every time a new moon passes in front of the sun. This does not occur every time in the moon's cycle, because the orbit of the moon is not in the same plane as Earth's path around the sun, so at most new moons, the moon passes either above or below the sun. However, occasionally, the new moon covers part of the sun or even all of it. If the sun is partially covered, the eclipse is called a partial eclipse. If the sun is totally covered, it is called a total eclipse. When an eclipse of the sun occurs, the moon casts a shadow onto Earth. People who are in this shadow can see the eclipse.

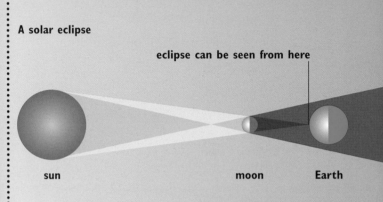

A solar eclipse

eclipse can be seen from here

sun   moon   Earth

LUNAR ECLIPSE

An eclipse of the moon occurs when the moon moves into a shadow cast into space by Earth. This happens up to three times a year, so lunar eclipses are more frequent than solar eclipses. Also, a lunar eclipse can be seen from anywhere on Earth, while a solar eclipse can be seen in only a few places.

A lunar eclipse

sun   Earth   moon

MAKE A SOLAR ECLIPSE

Place a globe on a table and hold a small ball in front of it. Ask a friend to shine a flashlight on the ball and look for the shadow cast on the globe. If you were In the shadow, you would see an eclipse. (You will need to do this in a dark room to best see the shadow.)

MAKE A LUNAR ECLIPSE

Place a globe on a table and hold a small ball behind it. Ask a friend to shine a flashlight on the globe and see how the ball is left in the shadow of the globe.

EATING UP THE SUN

Some ancient peoples did not make the connection between the movement of the sun and the movement of the moon. They thought that during a solar eclipse, the sun was being eaten up by a monster such as a dragon. They believed that when they asked the monster to let the sun go, it did so.

PREDICTING THE FUTURE

The Babylonians lived more than 2,500 years ago. They studied the movements of the sun, moon, and planets because they believed they could use this information to predict events on Earth.

The ancient Greeks inherited much of the Babylonians' knowledge, and it is believed that the Greek philosopher Thales used their data to predict an eclipse in 585 B.C. When it occurred as he predicted, a battle was stopped and the two armies made peace.

This is a Babylonian boundary stone. It shows the sun, moon, Venus, and some star constellations.

COMETS AND ASTEROIDS

Comets are large lumps of ice and dust that are mostly found beyond our solar system. But sometimes a comet moves close to the sun and develops a bright, luminous tail. Asteroids are rocks of all shapes and sizes. Most asteroids orbit the sun between Mars and Jupiter.

WHAT ARE COMETS?

The ancient Greeks thought that comets were clouds, but other people thought that they were a sign that a disaster was about to happen. Today, we know that a comet is a large lump of ice and dust that travels regularly from the edge of the solar system, around the sun, and then back again.

The sun releases huge numbers of tiny, fast-moving particles that move through space as solar wind. As a comet approaches the sun, some of the ice melts, and the gases that are released are pushed by the solar wind to form a tail behind the comet. Dust and grit released by the melting ice forms a second tail. The comet's tails always point away from the sun. This happens even when the comet is moving away from the sun, as the solar wind pushes the tails ahead of the main body of the comet. Comets eventually break up and form some of the meteors or shooting stars that pass through Earth's atmosphere.

HALLEY'S COMET

Edmund Halley (1656–1742), an English astronomer, observed the path of a comet in 1682. He compared the path with those of comets observed in the past. He found that the comets recorded in 1456, 1531, and 1607 seemed to have similar paths to the 1682 one. He also saw that the appearances of the comets were about 75 years apart. He had an idea that it was the same comet returning four times and predicted that it would return again in 1785. When it did, it was named Halley's Comet, and it has returned regularly ever since.

A comet seems to hover in the sky, but each night, its position changes.

This discovery led to the idea that comets can return many times to the sun. Halley's Comet last returned in 1986 and is due to approach the sun again in 2062. How old will you be then?

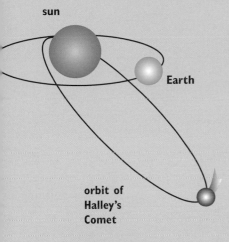

sun

Earth

orbit of
Halley's
Comet

MAKE A COMET

Make a comet from a pencil, a ball of clay, and some string. Move it toward and away from a fan or hair drier (which acts like the solar wind). When does the comet follow its tail?

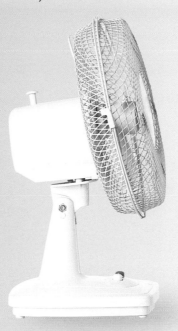

WHAT ARE ASTEROIDS?

Asteroids are rocks that move in an orbit around the sun. They range in size from grains of sand to huge chunks hundreds of miles across. Most asteroids occur in a ring, called the asteroid belt, between the orbits of Mars and Jupiter (see pages 12–13). Some asteroids have been found traveling with Jupiter in its orbit. A few have orbits that bend around the sun in a way that takes them across the orbit of Earth.

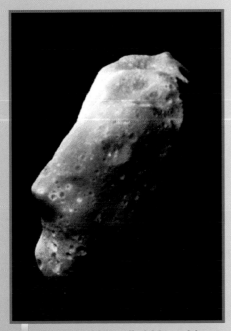

This asteroid is called Ida and has its own moon.

DISCOVERING THE ASTEROIDS

When scientists collect large amounts of information, they look for patterns that might help them make more discoveries. Johann Bode (1747–1826), a German astronomer, believed that there was a pattern in the distances of the planets from the sun. He found that there was a gap in the pattern between Mars and Jupiter, and astronomers began looking for a planet in this region. They never found one, but they did discover the asteroid belt.

TELESCOPES

Before the invention of the telescope, most people believed that objects in the heavens were perfect and that everything in space moved around Earth. Observations with a telescope, first made by Galileo, began to change people's minds.

It is thought that the telescope was invented in Holland in 1608. A year later, Galileo learned about it and made one for himself. He found that instead of being perfectly smooth, the moon had a rough surface with mountains, and that the sun had spots.

He went on to discover four moons in orbit around Jupiter (see above). This supported the work of Copernicus and Kepler, as it again indicated that not everything in space went around Earth. However, the Catholic Church based its teachings on the Greek ideas of an Earth-centered universe. It refused to accept Galileo's work, and the pope suppressed his books and had him imprisoned in his home for the last part of his life.

THE **REFRACTOR**

Galileo used a type of telescope called a refractor. It is made from two lenses placed at opposite ends of a tube. Light is bent, or refracted, by the lenses to make a magnified picture of the sky when observed through the eyepiece.

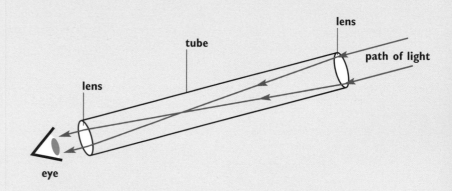

THE **REFLECTOR**
Sir Isaac Newton made a telescope in a different way. He used a curved mirror to collect light from the sky and then looked at it with a lens. This produced a brighter view because less light was absorbed as it passed through one lens instead of two. This type of telescope is called a reflector and is widely used today.

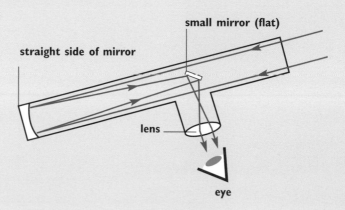

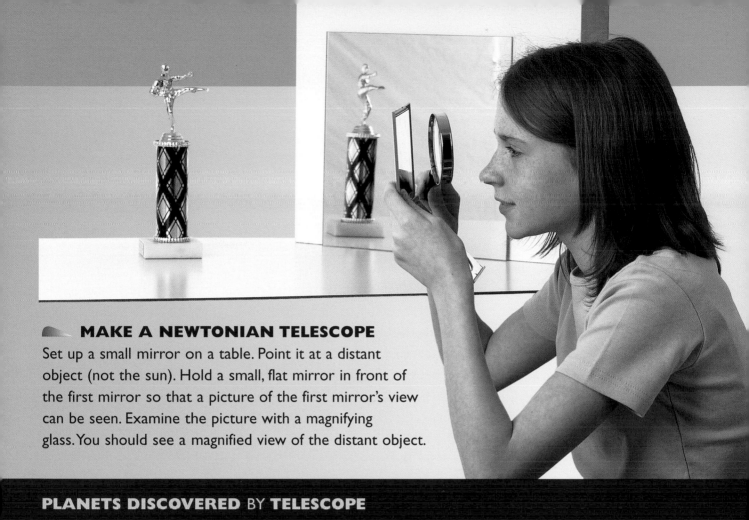

MAKE A NEWTONIAN TELESCOPE

Set up a small mirror on a table. Point it at a distant object (not the sun). Hold a small, flat mirror in front of the first mirror so that a picture of the first mirror's view can be seen. Examine the picture with a magnifying glass. You should see a magnified view of the distant object.

PLANETS DISCOVERED BY TELESCOPE

Before the telescope was invented and for some time after, people believed that there were just six planets—Mercury, Venus, Earth, Mars, Jupiter, and Saturn. William Herschel (1738–1822) and his sister Caroline (1750–1848) made their own reflector telescopes and used them to look into space.

The Herschels worked together observing and recording what they saw.

William found an object that did not appear as a point of light, like a star, but as a disk, like a planet. The planet was named Uranus.

When astronomers studied the movement of Uranus in its orbit, they found that it behaved as if it was being pulled by the gravity of another planet. A place was calculated where the mysterious planet could be, and when Johann Galle (1812–1910), a German astronomer, looked there, he found it. It was soon named Neptune. More observations suggested that Uranus and Neptune were being pulled by yet another planet. Clyde Tombaugh (1906–1997), an American astronomer, took many photographs through a telescope to find it. The planet was named Pluto.

STARS IN THE SKY

When you look at the stars, you are looking beyond the solar system and into deep space. It is here that all the stars in the universe, with the exception of the sun, are found.

DO CONSTELLATIONS EXIST?

When we look at the night sky from Earth, we can recognize groups of stars called constellations, many of which were first mapped and named by the Babylonians. These are just patterns of stars that we observe from our viewpoint on Earth. They do not really exist in deep space. Stars that appear to form a particular shape or constellation to us on Earth may in fact be many light-years apart. One may be 70 light-years away, while another could be more than 700 light-years away.

WHAT IS A LIGHT-YEAR?

The distances in deep space are so huge that the speed of light is used to measure them. The unit of distance is the light-year. It is the distance covered by a ray of light in a year and is 5.9 trillion miles (9.5 trillion km).

MAKE A CONSTELLATION

The stars in a constellation form a certain pattern only when viewed from Earth. If you looked at them from a different place, they would make a different pattern. Make a model constellation of three stars with three bulbs and three batteries. Look at them in the dark from different positions and see how they look.

A model constellation.

This is the constellation Orion. The distances of these stars from Earth range from 470 to 2,000 light-years. Can you see the three bright stars that form Orion's belt?

USING CONSTELLATIONS

Constellations allow astronomers to make a map of the sky and use it to communicate their discoveries. For example, if a comet appears, its position can be noted by looking at the constellation that is behind it. When other astronomers look in the direction of the constellation, they too will be able to find the comet.

WHAT IS A STAR?

A star is a huge ball of gas in space. It is formed by a combination of hydrogen and helium gases. The force of gravity that the ball of gas creates pulls in the gases and squashes them tightly together at the center of the ball. The squashing causes the hydrogen gas to change into helium gas in a process called nuclear fusion. Huge amounts of energy are released in this process. The energy passes through the gas ball and is released at its surface mainly as light and heat.

The amount of heat a star releases affects its color. The color order from coolest to hottest is red, orange, yellow, yellow-white, white, blue-white, and blue. The sun shines with a yellow light.

HOW **FAR AWAY** ARE THE **STARS?**

Friedrich Bessel (1784–1846), a German astronomer, measured the position of a star from two different places in Earth's orbit. The position of the star seemed to move against the stars in the background. This phenomenon is called parallax. Bessel used his measurements to calculate the distance of the star. He found it to be 350 trillion miles (560 trillion km) away.

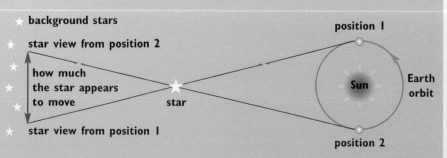

Other astronomers began to use parallax to find the distances of stars. They found that stars closer to Earth moved more against the background stars than stars that were farther away.

CAN YOU SEE THE STAR MOVE?

Hold up a cardboard star on a stick at arm's length. Look at it against a view from a window. Look at it with just your left eye, then just your right. Notice how far the star seems to move. Now move the star closer to your face and look at it again with each eye in turn. How does it appear to move now?

LOCAL STARS

The closest star to the sun is Alpha Centauri, which is just over four light-years away from the sun. Some stars are in pairs and are called double stars. A single or double star is called a star system; within 15 light-years of the sun, there are 23 star systems. The sun and its local stars form part of a much larger group of stars—a galaxy.

GALAXIES

About 15 billion years ago, the universe did not exist. Everything changed when a huge explosion called the Big Bang occurred, and the universe was formed.

The Big Bang caused the universe to grow, and as it did, it produced huge clouds of hydrogen and helium gas. Inside the clouds, the gases swirled around and formed millions of huge gas balls. The gravity of the gas balls compressed the gases, causing nuclear fusion at their centers that made them shine. They had become stars, and clouds of shining stars became galaxies. The galaxy we live in is called the Milky Way. There are millions of galaxies in the universe.

A spiral galaxy made up of gases, dust, stars, and planets.

THE MILKY WAY GALAXY

The Milky Way got its name from how it appears in the sky. It looks like a pale band of light stretching across the sky just like spilled milk looks when it flows across a black floor. The reason it appears like this is because we are looking along the edge of the galaxy. If you could look down on the galaxy, you would see that it has a bright center of many stars and spiral arms composed of stars. There are about 200 billion stars in the Milky Way, and it has a diameter of about 100,000 light-years.

This picture shows a cluster of galaxies.

GROUPS OF GALAXIES

The Milky Way is not the only galaxy in the universe. Galaxies cluster together into groups. The Milky Way is just one of 30 galaxies called the Local Group because they are the closest to Earth. Farther away, there are larger clusters, with thousands of galaxies in each one.

SHAPES OF GALAXIES

Not all galaxies are spiral-shaped. The most common type is elliptical, and the least common are those with an irregular shape.

GALAXIES ON THE MOVE

Galaxies move in space. The Milky Way moves like a slowly turning wheel, taking 225 million years to turn around once. All galaxies are moving away from each other due to the action of the Big Bang.

HOW GALAXIES MOVE AWAY

Inflate a balloon a little and draw galaxies on its surface with a felt tip pen. Now blow the balloon up to its full size and see how the galaxies move farther apart.

FINDING OTHER GALAXIES

At the beginning of the 20th century, it was believed that the Milky Way was in fact the universe. Gas clouds that were seen in it were thought to be part of the galaxy. Edwin Hubble (1889–1953), an American astronomer, used a new, large telescope to investigate some of these gas clouds and found that they were galaxies. This meant that the universe was much larger than scientists had thought.

The *Hubble Space Telescope (HST)* is named after Edwin Hubble. It was launched into orbit around Earth in 1990. The *HST* can look deeper into space than any other telescope on Earth.

SPACE MYSTERIES

Although we know a great deal about the universe, there is much more to find out. We know there is life on Earth, but what about in other parts of the solar system or on the planets that are being discovered around other stars? Could we go and live there too? Space probes carrying robots are investigating the solar system, and astronauts are examining ways to survive in space, while scientists continue to investigate the origins of the universe.

PROBABLE LIFE-FORMS

While there may be larger alien beings in other parts of the universe, scientists are looking for small forms of life, similar to microbes on Earth, in other parts of the solar system. In a recent visit to Mars by a space probe, the soil was tested for signs of life, but so far none have been found.

WATER AND LIFE

As far as we know, all living things need water to survive. So when explorations are made, scientists look for signs of water. On Europa, one of Jupiter's moons, there is a surface of ice. Scientists think that there may be an ocean of water underneath, and plans are being made to send a probe to Europa to drill through the ice and search the water for living things. Traces of water and salt have also been found on Mars by the recent probe *Opportunity*, and some scientists are optimistic that life will be found there.

TEST FOR SIGNS OF LIFE

Yeast is a microbe used to make bread. Mix some yeast with sand to see how scientists might investigate microbes in space. Add some sugar and water and stir up the contents. Then make another mixture of sand, sugar, and water, but no yeast. Put the two mixtures in a warm place for an hour, then look at both. Bubbles in the mixture indicate respiration—a sign of life. Which mixture produces bubbles?

Albert Einstein (1879–1955), a physicist born in Germany, developed the general theory of relativity to explain how matter and gravity are related in space. From this work, American scientist J. Robert Oppenheimer (1904–1967) calculated that if a star with a mass greater than 3.2 times that of the sun were to run out of hydrogen and collapse, it would produce an object with a force of gravity that was so great that not even light could escape from it. This object is called a black hole.

A black hole's gravity can also pull in material from other stars. Scientists are not sure what happens in a black hole, but some scientists believe that a black hole causes another big bang, which creates another universe. This means it is possible that our universe was created by a black hole in another universe.

SURVIVING IN SPACE

Spacesuits and spacecraft can help astronauts survive in space by giving them the warm, comfortable conditions found on Earth. But there is just one problem: Out in space, there is zero gravity, and our bodies—and the bodies of all living things—are adapted for life in the pulling of gravity at Earth's surface. How can we travel across space and take Earth life with us to set up new colonies? To answer this question, many investigations are taking place in conditions where the body seems weightless. These occur in space stations in orbit around Earth and in test aircraft that dive toward Earth and then land safely.

This astronaut seems to be weightless as he moves around in space above Earth.

HOW WEIGHT CHANGES

Ask an adult to cut the top off a large plastic bottle. Attach a heavy object, such as a ball of clay, to a rubber band and hang it from a pencil across the top of the bottle. Hold up the bottle and see how far the weight stretches the rubber band. Now lower the bottle quickly as if it were falling. You should see the rubber band get shorter as if the object inside was losing weight.

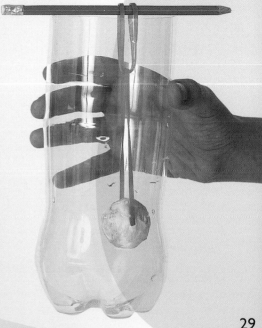

Thales (624–546 B.C.), a Greek philosopher, used data that had been collected about eclipses to predict one in 585 B.C.

Plato (427–347 B.C.), a Greek philosopher, believed that objects in the heavens, such as stars and planets, were set in crystal spheres.

Ptolemy (A.D. 90–168), a Greek astronomer, suggested that the planets move in small circles within their spheres.

William of Occam (1280–1349), an English monk, advised scientists to look for simple explanations for their observations rather than complicated ones.

Nicolaus Copernicus (1473–1543), a Polish astronomer, believed Ptolemy's idea was too complicated. He suggested that the sun was the center of the universe and that Earth moved in a path around the sun.

Tycho Brahe (1546–1601), a Danish astronomer, made a large number of observations of the heavens without a telescope. His data helped Kepler (see below).

Johannes Kepler (1571–1630), a German astronomer, used Brahe's data to show that the planets move in elliptical orbits around the sun.

Galileo (1564–1642), an Italian scientist, was the first person to use a telescope to make scientific observations of the heavens.

Sir Isaac Newton (1642–1727), an English scientist, described how objects in the solar system are moved by the pull of gravity between them.

Edmund Halley (1656–1742), an English astronomer, discovered that comets pass around the sun many times.

John Flamsteed (1646–1719), an English astronomer, observed stars from the Observatory at Greenwich in London and was honored by having the prime meridian of zero degrees on maps called the Greenwich Meridian.

John Harrison (1693–1776), an Englishman, invented a clock that could keep time as it traveled across the sea on a ship and help sailors with their navigation.

William Herschel (1738–1822) and his sister **Caroline (1750–1848)**, both British astronomers, made their own telescopes and used them to look into space. William discovered the planet Uranus.

Johann Bode (1747–1826), a German astronomer, studied the arrangement of the planets in the solar system, leading to the discovery of asteroids.

Friedrich Bessel (1784–1846), a German astronomer, used parallax to measure the distances to some nearby stars.

Johannn Galle (1812–1910), a German astronomer, discovered the planet Neptune.

Jean Foucault (1819–1868), a French physicist, showed that Earth turns by observing the swinging of a large pendulum.

John Tyndall (1820–1893), an Irish scientist, showed how particles in the air could make the sky blue.

Edwin Hubble (1889–1953), an American astronomer, discovered that there were many galaxies in the universe.

Clyde Tombaugh (1906–1997), an American astronomer, discovered the planet Pluto.

GLOSSARY

asteroids – pieces of rock in orbit around the sun, ranging in size from less than a millimeter to 600 miles (940 km) across.

astronomer – a scientist who studies objects in space.

axis – a line running through the center of Earth from the North to the South Pole. The planet turns around this line.

Babylonians – people who lived in Babylon (modern Iraq) 4,000 years ago.

comet – a large lump of rock and ice in orbit around the sun. When it is near the sun, it produces two tails.

equator – an imaginary line around the middle of Earth. It divides the Northern Hemisphere and the Southern Hemisphere.

gravity – a force that pulls any two objects in the universe toward each other.

hemisphere – either the northern or the southern half of Earth.

horizon – the line in the distance where the Earth and the sky seem to meet.

orbit – the path of a satellite or moon around a planet, and the path of a planet around the sun.

parallax – how the position of a star appears to move against the stars in the background when viewed from different positions.

pendulum – a weight on the end of a string or rope that swings to and fro.

planet – a large object made of rock or mainly gases that moves in a regular orbit around a star.

quadrant – an old instrument for measuring angles. It could be used to calculate the height of a planet in the sky by measuring the angle made between the object and the horizon.

respiration – the process of taking in oxygen and giving out carbon dioxide. This takes place when a living thing breathes.

satellite – a natural satellite is an object, like the moon, that moves around a planet. Artificial satellites are machines put into orbit around a planet to photograph space.

season – a period of the year that has a particular weather pattern, such as long, sunny days or short, cold days with rain or snow.

shadow – a dark area behind an object where light rays do not reach.

solar system – the sun and the objects—such as planets, asteroids, and comets—that move around it.

solar wind – a stream of electrically charged particles that spreads out from the sun in all directions.

space probe – a space vehicle that has no crew but carries scientific instruments and is sent from Earth to explore other parts of the solar system.

star – a huge, hot ball of gas in space that releases large amounts of energy as light and heat.

telescope – an instrument that makes distant objects appear much closer.

universe – all of space and all the objects in it.

INDEX